essentials
TOMATO

essentials

TOMATO

Exploit the versatility, aroma, and taste

Edited by Jane Donovan

CB
CONTEMPORARY BOOKS

With much love to Gary Connell and thanks for his culinary inspiration

A QUINTET BOOK

Published in the United States in 1999 by
Contemporary Books
A division of NTC/Contemporary Publishing Group, Inc.
4255 West Touhy Avenue
Lincolnwood (Chicago), Illinois 60712-1975 U.S.A.

ISBN 0-8092-2327-9

This book was designed and produced by
Quintet Publishing Limited
6 Blundell Street
London N7 9BH

Creative Director: Richard Dewing
Art Director: Paula Marchant
Designer: Isobel Gillan
Senior Editor: Clare Hubbard
Assistant Editor: Carine Tracanelli
Editor: Jane Donovan

Typeset in Great Britain by
Central Southern Typesetters, Eastbourne
Manufactured in Hong Kong by
Regent Publishing Services Ltd
Printed in China by
Leefung-Asco Printers Ltd

Library of Congress cataloging-in-publication data is available from the
United States Library of Congress

Material in this book has previously appeared in Quintet titles.

Note: Fresh herbs should be used in the recipes unless otherwise stated.

Titles also available in this series are *Chocolate* (ISBN 0-8092-2328-7) and *Egg* (ISBN 0-8092-2326-0).

CONTENTS

Introduction

tomatoes are the ultimate fast food. Today they are available in a range of different flavors, textures, and colors. Canned plum tomatoes (whole and chopped varieties), puréed tomatoes (passata), tomato pastes, and sun-dried tomatoes (dry or in olive oil) are also essential tomato-based products to have on hand in the kitchen, and they form the basis of many dishes. Although used as a vegetable, the tomato is actually a fruit. It was first grown as a decorative garden plant and was at one time considered too dangerous to eat, being related to the same family of plants as Deadly Nightshade. Nowadays tomatoes are consumed all year. From mid-spring through summer delicious home-grown tomatoes are available and interesting imported varieties, including yellow tomatoes, can be found at any time of year. When buying, choose firm tomatoes. ripe are best if they are to be eaten immediately and under-ripe are better for eating in a few days. For the best flavor, avoid refrigerating tomatoes. Sprinkle cherry tomatoes with sea salt and bake them in balsamic vinegar for about 10 minutes for a wonderful side salad, add the seeds to vegetable stocks to increase the flavor, or purée tomato flesh (add extra virgin olive oil, a splash of white wine vinegar, and a tablespoon of your favorite chopped herbs, then season) for a quick sauce served hot or cold. Experiment with the recipes and ideas in this book. Above all, enjoy tomatoes!

The flavors of tomatoes

On or off the vine, nothing beats the flavor and aroma of fresh tomatoes, especially when they are home-grown. Purchase different varieties to add texture, taste, and color to your cooking. To retain the best flavor and for an attractive display in the kitchen, store them in a shallow bowl. Shown here are some of the most popular varieties:

3

3 tuscan vine tomatoes can be cut and rubbed on bruschetta which is then seasoned with sea salt and olive oil.

1 beefsteak (bullock) tomatoes are large, extremely tasty, and perfect for baking or served cold with various fillings, such as flavored mayonnaise or cream cheese.

green tomatoes are deliciously tangy in chutneys, pickles, and relishes.

2 plum (roma) tomatoes, rich red in color, these juicy tomatoes are ideal for cooking.

5 cherry tomatoes, sweet, tiny, and crisp.

6 globe tomatoes are medium-sized and are good both raw and cooked.

4 yellow pear and hot-house tomatoes add interesting shapes and extra color to all kinds of dishes.

Specialist **tomato** products

Specialist tomato products (available in delicatessens and supermarkets) will add zest to your cooking and are essential ingredients for every pantry. Keep these items on hand and you will be able to quickly transform all kinds of sauces, soups, and salads, and create flavorful snacks, as well as main course dishes. Shown here are some of the tomato products that you will find useful:

2 canned plum tomatoes
are the basis of many sauces.

1 sun-dried tomatoes

packed in oil in jars are rich and salty in flavor which works well when served with cheeses and breads, chopped in dressings and dips, and loose with fresh pasta or in salads.

3 salsa

is available to buy fresh, canned, or in jars and can range from mild to very hot.

3

passata

is a useful base for sauces and soups; store in the refrigerator.

4 ketchups

and relishes, homemade or commercial, are useful accompaniments to many main recipes.

5 tomato pastes

, sun-dried and ordinary—thinly spread on toasted crostini, tomato paste makes a superb appetizer and it can also be used for an instant pizza topping.

4

5

7 tomato purée

is great to use in pasta sauces.

6

7

6 dry sun-dried tomatoes—

reconstitute them in boiling water and marinate or use them in recipes.

Cooking Techniques

For some of the recipes in this book, the tomatoes need to be prepared in advance. Here are some basic techniques to get you started.

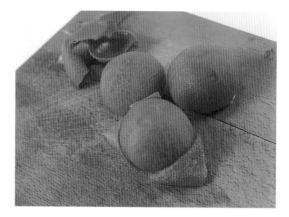

Skinning & Seeding Tomatoes

Rinse the tomatoes then place them in a large heatproof bowl. Cover with boiling water and let stand for 30 to 60 seconds depending on their ripeness. Drain, slit lightly with a sharp knife, and peel away the skins. To seed tomatoes, halve or quarter them and use a teaspoon to scoop out the seeds.

Diced Tomatoes

This technique is also known as *concassé*. Skin and seed the tomatoes (see above), then cut them into small squares (dice). Diced tomatoes form the basis of many sauces, soups, salsas, and stuffings.

Roast Tomatoes

The following recipe is delicious served with crusty bread to soak up the juices. Capers, olives, or anchovies can be scattered on top, for a salty Mediterranean flavor.

SERVES **4**

12 small to medium-sized ripe flavorful tomatoes
4 to 5 Tbsp extra virgin olive oil
½ to 1 tsp balsamic vinegar, or to taste
Coarse sea salt to taste
3 to 5 garlic cloves, chopped fine
Handful of basil, coarsely torn

Arrange the tomatoes in a casserole, about an inch or so apart, and drizzle with about 1 to 2 teaspoons of the olive oil.

Preheat the oven to 425°F and roast the tomatoes for 20 minutes. Reduce the heat to 325°F and continue to cook for a further 30 minutes. The skins should be darkened and cracked. Remove from the oven and let cool, preferably overnight so their juices can thicken.

Remove the skins from the tomatoes and squeeze any remaining juices from the skins, letting the juices run back onto the tomatoes.

Serve at room temperature, drizzled with olive oil, and balsamic vinegar, and sprinkled with salt, garlic, and basil.

Home-dried Tomatoes

These preserved tomatoes can be used to enliven all kinds of dishes. Store them in plain or flavored olive oil.

MAKES ABOUT **2** LB

2 lb ripe tomatoes
1 tsp salt
1 tsp sugar
About 2 cups olive oil

Preheat the oven to 250°F. Wash and dry the tomatoes, discarding any that are damaged.

Cut the tomatoes in half, scoop out the seeds, and sprinkle the cut surfaces with salt and sugar. Place, cut side down, onto a cooling rack and place in oven. Place a baking sheet on shelf below cooling rack to catch any drips. Insert a skewer in the oven door so that it is slightly ajar and leave the tomatoes for 6 hours.

Pack into sterilized jars, cover with olive oil, and seal. Use within 6 months.

Sun-dried Plum Tomatoes

Here is another simple way of preserving tomatoes. Just wash, dry, and halve 12 plum tomatoes. Remove the seeds (see page 12) and core the tomatoes. Place on a baking sheet lined with aluminum foil, add a few chopped garlic cloves and some thyme sprigs. Sprinkle with a little salt and sugar and drizzle with olive oil. Bake in a preheated oven (250°F) for 3½ hours. Allow to cool, then soak in a sterilized glass jar filled with olive oil. The tomatoes will keep for 10 to 12 days in the refrigerator.

TOMATO GARNISHES

Use tomatoes as a garnish for mousses, pâtés, and terrines, almost any cold meat, fish or vegetable dish, and egg recipes. Try the following ideas:

Tomato Waterlily

Choose medium-sized, firm, ripe tomatoes. With a sharp knife and working horizontally around the middle of the tomato, cut zigzags all the way round to produce a jagged line.

Pull the two tomato halves apart carefully to produce two waterlily shapes and decorate with chopped fine parsley or chives.

Tomato Rose

Select medium-sized, firm, ripe tomatoes. With a small, sharp paring knife and starting at the non-stalk end of the tomato, slice a continuous paper-thin strip of skin ½ inch wide, and cut in a circular fashion around the tomato to produce a spiral.

Using the stem end of the strip to form the center of the rose, carefully wind the tomato peel around itself, skin side out.

When completely wound, shape the skin into a rose, making "petals" more open around the base of the flower. A couple of bay or mint leaves adds the final touch.

 THE BASICS

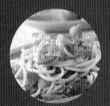

Andalusian Tomato Vinaigrette

*Tomato vinaigrette is especially
good tossed with garbanzo beans
or with broiled artichokes.*

SERVES **4**

2 to 3 large garlic cloves
Salt to taste
3 ripe tomatoes (canned are fine)
1 Tbsp balsamic vinegar
1 Tbsp sherry vinegar
Pinch of oregano
About 6 Tbsp extra virgin olive oil

Using a mortar and pestle, grind the garlic with
the salt until it forms a paste. Dice the tomatoes
(see page 12) and work them into the mixture.

Add the vinegars and the oregano, then slowly
add the olive oil until the mixture forms a vinaigrette.

Serving Ideas

- *Toss the vinaigrette in a mixture of sturdy and delicate
  leaves. Add a good scattering of fresh herbs,
  such as tarragon, chervil, chives, and shallots.*
- *Charbroil eggplant slices, zucchini, and bell peppers,
  then toss in vinaigrette and serve warm.*
- *Sprinkle onto peeled and blanched baby fava beans,
  along with a shower of thinly shaved Parmesan or
  Romano cheese.*

Fresh Tomato Sauce

When making tomato sauce, look for tomatoes that are properly ripened but not over-ripe. For a truly authentic taste, use plum tomatoes.

MAKES 2½ CUPS

1½ lb tomatoes
½ small fennel bulb (about 2 Tbsp chopped)
3 Tbsp olive oil
1 onion, peeled and chopped
2 to 3 garlic cloves, peeled and crushed
Few sprigs of oregano
2 to 3 Tbsp tomato paste
1¼ cups vegetable broth
Salt and ground black pepper

Skin the tomatoes (see page 12), cut in half and chop roughly. Trim the fennel, discarding any damaged outer leaves, then chop fine.

Heat the oil in a heavy saucepan and gently sauté the fennel, onion, and garlic for 5 minutes or until soft but not browned. Add the chopped tomatoes with the oregano sprigs and sauté for another 3 minutes.

Blend the tomato paste with a little vegetable broth, then add to the pan with the remaining broth. Bring to a boil and let simmer for 10 to 12 minutes or until reduced to a sauce consistency. Remove the oregano sprigs and season to taste.

Serving Ideas

- Toss lightly with 1 pound fresh pasta (boiled in salted water just until tender); top with 1 to 2 teaspoons freshly chopped oregano.
- Broil fresh salmon and serve warmed sauce on the side with salad leaves.
- Make a filling of goat cheese, mint, and spinach. Place some filling in the center of phyllo pastry squares and roll up (seal with water). Brush with egg and bake in the oven until golden brown. Serve the sauce on the side.
- Mix the sauce with gnocchi or tortellini stuffed with ricotta and top with freshly grated Parmesan and ground black pepper.
- Preheat the oven to 400°F. Slice eggplants about ½ inch thick. Brush a baking sheet with a little olive oil and layer the slices on top. Brush the eggplant slices generously with oil. Sprinkle with fresh thyme and add salt and ground black pepper. Bake until tender, about 15 to 20 minutes. Spread the slices with the tomato sauce, add plenty of Parmesan, and return to the oven until the cheese bubbles.

Pizza Napolitana

The pizza dough can be stored in the refrigerator for about a week if you wish to make it up in advance.

MAKES I LARGE PIZZA

PIZZA DOUGH

¾ cup warm water (105 to 115°F—it should
   feel slightly hotter than your wrist)

½ package active, dry yeast

I tsp sugar

¼ cup extra virgin olive oil

I lb strong, white flour

I cup whole wheat flour

I tsp salt

TOPPING

Tomato paste

I red onion, sliced thin

About 6 very ripe, flavorful tomatoes, diced (see page 12)

About 5 canned or fresh anchovies, diced

5 to 10 oil-cured olives, pitted and halved

2 round fresh mozzarella, thinly sliced

I tsp capers

2 garlic cloves, chopped fine

3 to 4 Tbsp olive oil

I Tbsp oregano leaves, chopped fine

Freshly shredded Parmesan and red hot-pepper flakes,
   to serve

🍅 Combine the water with the yeast and sugar. When it starts to foam, after 5 to 10 minutes, add the olive oil. Combine the flours and set aside about a cupful of this mixture. Mix the remainder with the salt in a big bowl. Make a well and pour the liquid into it. Work the mixture into a dough.

🍅 Dust your hands and a board with the leftover flour. Turn the dough out onto it. Knead until the dough is smooth and elastic with an almost satin sheen. You will need to keep flouring the board and your hands. After 10 minutes the dough will spring back when you press a finger into it.

🍅 Place the dough in a large, oiled bowl to rise and cover with a damp cloth or plastic wrap. Leave in a warm place for about 90 minutes; then punch the dough down and let it rise again; this time it will rise more quickly and will be easier to work with.

🍅 Preheat the oven to 400 to 450°F. Arrange the dough on a baking sheet or pizza pan. Spread with a thin layer of tomato paste, the red onion, diced tomatoes, anchovies, and olives. Add fresh mozzarella, capers, and garlic.

🍅 Drizzle the pizza with olive oil, sprinkle with oregano, and bake for 15 to 25 minutes. Serve with Parmesan and red hot-pepper flakes, as desired.

Tomato Salsa

Serve this salsa in a small bowl with a selection of chopped raw vegetables and tortilla chips.

SERVES **4**

2 red jalapeño chillies, seeded and chopped fine

6 scallions, chopped fine

8 oz ripe tomatoes

2 garlic cloves

2 Tbsp cilantro, chopped fine

2 Tbsp lime juice

2 Tbsp olive oil

Salt and ground black pepper

1 ripe avocado

Place the chillies in a bowl with the scallions. Peel, seed, and finely chop the tomatoes (see page 12) and crush the garlic.

Add the tomatoes and garlic to the bowl, together with the cilantro, lime juice, and oil. Season, cover, and leave for 30 minutes. Peel, pit, and chop the avocado; add it to the sauce and serve immediately.

Chili Tomato Dip

A simple yet delicious appetizer that is quick to prepare.

SERVES **4**

Selection of fresh vegetables, trimmed and cut into strips or small pieces (try celery sticks, bell peppers, carrots, cherry tomatoes, and snow peas)

1¼ cups plain yogurt

1 Tbsp tomato paste

4 Tbsp low-fat mayonnaise

1 green chili, seeded and chopped fine

1 Tbsp parsley, chopped fine

Prepare the vegetables. Mix together the dip ingredients and place in a serving bowl.

Place the bowl on a serving platter and arrange the vegetables around the dip. Serve immediately.

Serving Idea

- *For a low-fat lunch, fill a baked potato with Chili Tomato Dip or salsa.*

Tomato Tapenade

Tapenade is a famous spread that can be found throughout the Mediterranean.

SERVES **4**

8 oz black olives, pitted
6 sun-dried tomatoes
1½ oz capers (soaked if preferred)
1 Tbsp parsley, chopped fine
2 garlic cloves, crushed
1 tsp wholegrain mustard
2-oz can anchovy fillets (soaked if preferred)
½ cup extra virgin olive oil
Ground black pepper

Blend the olives, sun-dried tomatoes, capers, parsley, garlic, mustard, and anchovies with their oil to a thick paste in a food processor.

With the motor still running, gradually pour in the olive oil in a thin, steady stream to form a thick purée. Add black pepper to taste.

Serving Idea

• *Tapenade is traditionally served on toasted bread but it can also form the basis of an interesting salad to serve four. Cook 8 ounces fresh pasta, such as mixed herb farfalle, in plenty of salted boiling water for 1 to 2 minutes until* al dente. *Drain and return to the pan. Rinse a romaine lettuce and a few sprigs of watercress; use them to line a salad bowl. Add the tapenade to the cooked pasta and toss lightly. Serve in the lettuce-lined bowl, sprinkled with croutons and garnish with cherry tomatoes.*

Tomato Pilau

Press the pilau into small ramekins, then turn them out onto plates. Garnish with fresh herbs and serve as an accompaniment to grilled chicken or oven-roasted lamb.

SERVES **4**

2 leeks

2 Tbsp oil

2 garlic cloves, crushed

1 tsp ground coriander

½ tsp ground cinnamon

2 green bell peppers, seeded and chopped

6 oz basmati rice

1 Tbsp tomato paste

1 lb tomatoes

1¼ cups vegetable broth

Salt and ground black pepper

Herbs to garnish

Trim and slice the leeks. Sauté in oil with the garlic for 3 minutes. Add the spices and sauté for 2 minutes, then add the bell peppers and rice and cook for 3 minutes.

Blend the tomato paste in 2 tablespoons water; add to the pan. Peel and chop the tomatoes (see page 12). Add to the pan with the broth, then simmer, covered, for 25 minutes, stirring occasionally. Season, garnish with fresh herbs and serve.

Mediterranean Dressing

This dressing is full of the heat-soaked flavors of the Mediterranean.

MAKES ABOUT 1 CUP

2 oil-soaked sun-dried tomatoes
1 small garlic clove
1 Tbsp capers
About 8 black olives, pitted
1½ Tbsp red or white wine vinegar
7 Tbsp extra virgin olive oil
Ground black pepper

🍅 Finely chop the tomatoes, garlic, capers, and olives.

🍅 Place them in a bowl and add the vinegar. Slowly pour in the oil, whisking constantly, until well emulsified. Season with black pepper.

Serving Ideas

- *Serve the Tomato Pilau in the center of individual serving plates. Sprinkle with fresh herbs and drizzle Fresh Tomato Sauce (see page 18) around the edge of the plates for a light appetizer.*
- *Make a salad from cubed firm white bread (flavored with herbs or garlic if desired) and crisp salad leaves. Toss in a bowl with Mediterranean Dressing to taste.*
- *Spoon Mediterranean Dressing over broiled cheese topping or toss it with pasta.*

BITE-SIZE PIECES

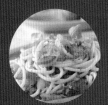

Oysters Bloody Mary

These piquant oysters are perfect for parties and they can also be served as a light appetizer.

SERVES **4**

1½ cups tomato juice
3 Tbsp vodka
5 drops Tabasco sauce
1 tsp Worcestershire sauce
1 Tbsp lemon juice
Salt and ground black pepper
12 fresh oysters
Diced cucumber
Diced small, young celery stalks
Lemon wedges, to serve

Mix a Bloody Mary using the tomato juice, vodka, Tabasco and Worcestershire sauces, lemon juice, and seasoning. Place these ingredients in a blender with some ice cubes so that it is well chilled.

Open the oysters carefully. To do this, slide an oyster knife into the back of the shell; sever the hinge close to the flat upper shell. Remove the upper shell and discard.

Cut the oyster from the lower shell and pick out any pieces of shell or grit. Place the cleaned oyster in the lower shell.

Fill the shells with the Bloody Mary mix and sprinkle cucumber and celery over the top. Serve immediately with lemon wedges.

Roasted Tomato Tartlets

When made with full-flavored, ripe tomatoes, these tartlets are fabulous.
The success of this dish lies in its simplicity.

SERVES **6**

DOUGH

2 cups fine whole wheat flour

1½ oz sesame seeds

½ tsp salt

1 large egg, beaten

¼ cup olive oil

About 3 to 4 Tbsp water

3 onions, sliced fine

2 garlic cloves, halved

3 Tbsp fruity olive oil, plus extra for brushing

3 to 4 sprigs thyme

2 bay leaves

Salt and ground black pepper

4 to 5 large tomatoes, sliced

Mix together the flour, sesame seeds, and salt, then make a well in the center. Add the egg and olive oil and mix to a soft dough, adding water as necessary. Divide the mixture into six equal parts and shape to line six 4-inch individual tart pans; this is more of a dough than a pastry and is easiest to mold into shape with your fingers. Chill the tart shells for at least 30 minutes while preparing the filling.

Cook the onions and garlic in the olive oil with the thyme and bay leaves for 30 to 40 minutes, until well softened and reduced. Season to taste with salt and pepper, then remove the herbs.

Preheat the oven to 425°F. Fill the tart shells with the onion mixture then top with the tomatoes, overlapping the slices and brushing them lightly with olive oil. Season well, then bake for 20 to 25 minutes until the dough is crisp and the tomatoes are just starting to blacken. Serve hot or cold with a small salad of mixed greens.

Sun-dried Tomatoes & Yellow Bell Peppers

This appetizer is delicious on small pieces of French bread or crisp crostini-like toasts.

SERVES **4**

3 yellow bell peppers, cut into bite-sized pieces

4 to 5 Tbsp extra virgin olive oil

4 to 5 garlic cloves, chopped fine

14 oz ripe tomatoes, diced (see page 12)

Pinch sugar

Salt and ground black pepper

8 to 10 marinated sun-dried tomatoes,
    cut into quarters

1 Tbsp balsamic vinegar or to taste

2 to 3 capers, rinsed and drained

Chopped parsley to garnish

Sauté the peppers in the olive oil for about 7 minutes until lightly brown but not too soft. Add half the garlic, the tomatoes, sugar, and seasoning, and cook over high heat until the tomatoes reduce to a thick paste.

Stir in the sun-dried tomatoes, balsamic vinegar, capers, and remaining garlic. Let cool to room temperature to serve. Garnish with parsley.

Red Pepper & Tomato Soufflés

SERVES **4**

COULIS

1 onion, chopped fine

1 Tbsp extra virgin olive oil

3 to 4 garlic cloves, chopped fine

2 red bell peppers, chopped fine

2 fresh or canned tomatoes, diced (see page 12)

¼ cup tomato juice mixed with ¼ cup water (optional)

Salt and ground black pepper

Pinch cayenne pepper or Tabasco sauce, to taste

Pinch sugar, to taste

Large pinch of your favorite herbs (try thyme,
    marjoram, or herbes de Provence)

Butter for individual soufflé molds

5 to 6 Tbsp grated Parmesan

6 eggs, at room temperature, separated

Large pinch salt

1 batch coulis (see above and method)

🍓 Make the coulis: in a heavy saucepan, lightly sauté the onion in olive oil until softened, then add the garlic and peppers. Continue to cook until softened. Add the tomatoes, cover, and cook until the mixture becomes a sauce. Add the tomato juice and water and bring to a boil. Cook for about 5 minutes or until soft, stirring continuously. Let cool and purée, then season with salt, pepper, cayenne or Tabasco, sugar, and herbs. Set aside until needed.

🍓 Preheat the oven to 425°F. Butter the molds generously and coat well with the grated cheese. Set aside.

🍓 Whisk the egg whites with the salt to form stiff, glossy peaks. Then whisk the yolks with half the coulis. Stir a large spoonful of the whites into the egg yolk and coulis mixture, then fold the mixture into the whites. Gently pour or spoon this into the prepared molds.

🍓 Bake for 15 to 20 minutes or until the soufflés are puffed up and slightly golden. Only open the oven door gently and briefly to check the soufflés or they will collapse. Serve immediately with the remaining coulis on the side.

Grilled Eggplant with Tomato & Mozzarella Cheese

These delightful eggplant packets, with a top accent of fresh basil, are great cooked on the grill.

SERVES **8**

1 large eggplant, weighing about 1 lb
Olive oil, for brushing
8 oz mozzarella cheese
2 large tomatoes
Salt and ground black pepper
8 sprigs of basil

🍆 Trim the stalk from the eggplant and cut lengthwise into 8 slices, each about ¼ inch thick, discarding the ends. Lightly brush both sides of each slice with olive oil. Slice the cheese into eight pieces and cut the tomatoes into eight slices, discarding the tops.

🍆 Cook one side of the eggplant slices over medium-high heat for about 3 minutes until lightly charred and soft. Place the eggplant, grilled sides up, on a large plate. Season lightly. Place a slice of cheese at one end, top with a tomato slice and then a basil sprig. Fold the eggplant over to make a small packet. Secure with a small, presoaked toothpick.

🍆 Cook over a medium-high heat for 3 to 4 minutes, turning once, until lightly charred. Serve immediately.

Serving Idea

- *This recipe could be part of a Mediterranean menu for a barbecue party. Try serving it with grilled meats, a flavorful mixed salad, and pieces of warm crusty bread to mop up the juices. Serve fresh fruit for dessert.*

Artichoke Hearts with Tomatoes & Lemon

A light tapas dish that is good with crusty bread and a tomato salad.

SERVES **4**

6 artichokes
Juice of 4 lemons
1 tsp flour
2½ cups cold water
Salt
¾ stick butter
1 small onion, chopped fine
1 tsp garlic, crushed
4 pieces smoked ham, chopped fine
8-oz can plum tomatoes
2 Tbsp parsley, chopped fine
Salt and ground black pepper

First prepare the artichokes. Trim away the stalks and pull out the leaves underneath. Cut through each artichoke, leaving only about an inch at the base. While holding the artichoke upside down, peel carefully with a small paring knife. Remove all the leaves and green part, keeping the base as smooth as possible. Rub with the juiced lemon and then place in a bowl of water with the juice of 1 lemon.

Remove the furry center chokes with a teaspoon and discard. Mix the flour and water, then add the salt and juice of 1 lemon. Pass through a strainer into a heavy saucepan and bring to a boil, stirring constantly. Add the artichokes. Let simmer gently until just tender, about 20 minutes. Drain.

Cut five or six triangles into the artichoke bottoms by cutting each one in half, then each half into two or three. Melt the butter in a heavy saucepan. Add the onion, garlic, and ham and cook gently for 5 minutes.

Add the tomatoes and parsley. Season and bring to a boil. Pour in the juice of 2 lemons.. Add the artichoke pieces. Heat gently, stirring. If the mix is too tart, add a pinch of sugar. Serve warm.

Stuffed Tomatoes

You can use small or large tomatoes for this recipe, which is very simple and a colorful addition to any table.

SERVES **4**

8 small or 3 large tomatoes
4 hard-cooked eggs, cooled and peeled
¾ cup garlic mayonnaise
Salt and ground black pepper
1 Tbsp chopped parsley
1 Tbsp white bread crumbs for the large tomatoes
Chopped parsley to garnish

Skin the tomatoes. Slice off the tops and just enough of their bases to remove the rounded ends so that the tomatoes will sit squarely on the plate. Keep the tops if using small tomatoes, but not for the large tomatoes.

Remove the seeds and insides, either with a teaspoon or a small, sharp knife.

Mash the eggs with the mayonnaise, salt, pepper, and the parsley.

Fill the tomatoes, firmly pressing down the filling. With small tomatoes, replace the lids at a jaunty angle. If keeping to serve later, brush them with olive oil and black pepper to prevent them from drying out. Cover with plastic wrap and keep in the refrigerator.

For large tomatoes, the filling must be very firm, so it can be sliced. If you make your own mayonnaise, thicken it by using more egg yolks. If you use store-bought mayonnaise, add enough white bread crumbs until the mixture is the consistency of mashed potatoes. Season well, to taste. Fill the tomatoes, pressing down firmly until level. Refrigerate for 1 hour, then slice with a sharp knife into rings. Sprinkle with chopped parsley.

Bruschetta

Serve this bright red mixture of roasted tomatoes and peppers on crispy toasted bread that has been rubbed with a garlic clove.

SERVES **4** TO **6**

4 small to medium-sized tomatoes
Pinch sugar
Salt
2 Tbsp extra virgin olive oil
4 red bell peppers, roasted, peeled, and diced
2 to 3 garlic cloves, chopped fine
Ground black pepper, to taste
Few drops of white wine or balsamic vinegar, to taste
Few basil leaves, torn (or try marjoram or oregano)

 Cut the tomatoes in half crosswise. Sprinkle the cut halves lightly with sugar and a tiny amount of salt.

 Heat a tablespoon of the olive oil in a heavy skillet just large enough to take all the tomato halves. When the skillet is hot, place the tomatoes skin-side down and cook for a few minutes over high heat until they are charred underneath. Turn the tomatoes over carefully, reduce the heat to medium-high, and cook, covered, until soft. Do not overcook. Remove from the heat and leave, covered, until cool.

 Dice the roasted tomatoes and combine them, with their juices, with the diced peppers and chopped garlic. Season and add the white wine or balsamic vinegar and remaining olive oil. Serve at room temperature, sprinkled with herbs.

ON THE SIDE

Andalusian Chopped-Vegetable Salad

*When the weather is hot, make up large quantities of this salad and serve it chilled
for any and every kind of meal—even breakfast, when it is exquisitely refreshing.*

SERVES **4**

1 large cucumber, diced

3 to 5 small, ripe tomatoes, diced (see page 12)

1 carrot, diced

1 red bell pepper, diced

1 green bell pepper, diced (add a yellow or orange
    bell pepper here, too, if desired)

1 small onion, chopped fine

3 to 5 garlic cloves, crushed

¼ tsp ground cumin or cumin seeds

Salt to taste

Juice of 1 lemon

1 tsp sherry vinegar or white wine vinegar

3 Tbsp extra virgin olive oil

Combine the cucumber, tomatoes, carrot, bell
peppers, onion, and garlic. Toss with cumin, salt, lemon,
sherry or white wine vinegar, and olive oil. Taste for
seasoning and chill until ready to eat.

Serving Ideas

- *Use the salad as a tasty relish in a* bocadillo *(a crusty Spanish-style sandwich) or serve with fresh broiled fish.*
- *Serve as a continental breakfast or brunch with a selection of cold meats and cheeses.*
- *Try the chopped-vegetable salad with dips and different breads for a light lunch.*

Tomato, Pumpkin, & Eggplant Salad

Serve this salad warm or cold, on a bed of arugula leaves, with plenty of Italian flat bread.

SERVES **4**

8 slices from a small pumpkin, each about
 ¾-in thick, deseeded
1 eggplant, quartered lengthwise
2 large tomatoes, halved
6 to 8 garlic cloves, unpeeled
Salt and ground black pepper
6 to 8 basil leaves, torn in half
Sugar
Olive oil
Basil leaves, to garnish
Olive oil bread, to serve

DRESSING
6 Tbsp extra virgin olive oil
1 Tbsp balsamic or sherry vinegar
1 tsp Dijon mustard
Pinch of sugar
1 tsp chopped arugula or 1 Tbsp chopped parsley

🍅 Preheat a 425°F oven. Arrange the prepared vegetables with the garlic in a roasting pan, then season with salt and pepper. Push the basil leaves into the flesh of the tomatoes, then scatter over a little sugar. Drizzle everything with olive oil, then roast at the top of the oven for 40 to 45 minutes, until the vegetables are just starting to blacken. (Check after 30 minutes and remove the tomatoes if they are already soft.)

🍅 Allow the vegetables to cool slightly, then cut the pumpkin away from the skin. Leave for 10 minutes if you intend to serve the salad warm, or until completely cold.

🍅 Prepare the dressing by blending all the ingredients together and season with salt, pepper, and sugar to taste.

🍅 Peel the garlic, then arrange the vegetables on serving plates. Pour the dressing over and then add a little basil to each helping. Serve immediately with plenty of olive oil bread.

Two-tomato Salsa

This salsa combines sweet cherry tomatoes with aromatic sun-dried tomatoes. Olive oil and basil are added for a true Mediterranean flavor.

SERVES **6**

8 oz sun-dried tomatoes in oil, drained

8 oz cherry tomatoes, halved

6 large scallions, sliced thin

2 Tbsp olive oil

2 Tbsp balsamic vinegar

1 tsp superfine sugar

Handful of basil leaves

Chop the sun-dried tomatoes and place in a large bowl with the cherry tomatoes. Add the sliced scallions.

Whisk together the oil, vinegar, and sugar. Pour over the tomatoes, toss to coat well then cover and chill for 1 hour.

Just before serving, tear the basil leaves into shreds and stir into the salsa.

Salsa Cruda

This classic, chunky mixture of chillies and a few flavorings defines Mexican cuisine around the world and is very healthful as well.

SERVES **4** TO **6**

3 to 5 jalapeño chillies, chopped fine
1 mild green chili
3 scallions, chopped fine
5 garlic cloves, chopped
3 to 5 ripe flavorful tomatoes, diced (see page 12)
Pinch sugar
¼ tsp cumin, or more to taste
Salt to taste
5 to 6 Tbsp chopped cilantro
Juice of ½ lemon or lime

🍅 Combine the chillies with the scallions, garlic, and tomatoes, then season with the sugar, cumin, and salt.

🍅 Toss with the cilantro and lemon or lime juice and taste for seasoning. Serve immediately or chill until ready to serve, preferably the same day.

Serving Ideas

- *Serve salsa with any kind of taco or tortilla chips and a selection of chopped, raw vegetables.*
- *Pan-fry a small selection of fish and seafood (try cod or other white fish strips, baby squid, and shrimp) in olive oil and lime juice. Season with ground black pepper and serve with salsa as a light appetizer.*

Bulgur-wheat Pilaf

A plate of this pilaf often forms part of a traditional Greek meze dinner. You really do need good, fresh tomatoes for this dish.

SERVES **4**

1 medium-large or 2 small onions, chopped

2 garlic cloves, chopped

3 medium-sized, ripe tomatoes, peeled and diced (see page 12)

2 Tbsp extra virgin olive oil

Handful of vermicelli, broken into small pieces (about 1 oz)

2 cups bulgur or cracked wheat

1½ cups vegetable or chicken broth, as desired

Salt, ground black pepper, and crushed, dried oregano leaves, to taste

Lightly sauté the onion, garlic, and tomatoes in the olive oil until softened, then stir in the vermicelli. It should be of a sautéeing consistency rather than a sauce consistency, so add extra olive oil, if needed.

Add the bulgur or cracked wheat, stir, then add the broth, salt, pepper, and oregano. Cover and cook over low heat until the broth is absorbed and the wheat is chewy and tender, about 8 to 10 minutes.

Leave the pilaf to sit a few minutes, then fluff it up with a fork and serve immediately.

Meze Dishes

Perhaps the most famous feature of Greek cuisine, meze means a small tidbit of food, something delicious to accompany a cool drink as you sit back and relax in the Mediterranean sunshine, chatting with friends and passers-by. In Greece, meze is served at every café, in every house, and on street corners. It can be anything from a small nibble of toasted pumpkin seeds to a whole array of tempting salads, dishes using a variety of savory pulses, dips, tiny kabobs, vegetables—stuffed and unstuffed—and much, much more, creating a mass of color, tastes, and textures, all chosen to complement and enhance each other.

Create your own meze table by choosing a selection of your favorite dishes, scaled-down. Serve the dishes a few at a time, beginning with the appetizer meze, followed by the main course dishes and finishing with sweet meze.

Tomato Rice

This is a popular Portuguese rice dish. Much of its character comes from the well-flavored tomatoes, so select carefully.

SERVES **4**

2 Tbsp olive oil
1 large onion, chopped fine
1 garlic clove, chopped fine
2 ripe, well-flavored tomatoes, skinned, seeded, and chopped fine
1 cup long-grain rice
2½ cups boiling water
2 Tbsp chopped parsley
Salt and ground black pepper

🍅 Heat the oil in a heavy saucepan, add the onion and garlic, and fry until softened but not brown.

🍅 Stir in the tomatoes, and cook for a further 5 minutes or so before adding the rice. Stir to coat the vegetables with the rice, then add the boiling water. Bring to a boil, cover, and cook over low heat until the rice is tender and all the liquid has been absorbed. Stir in the parsley and season to taste.

Serving Ideas

- *Serve the rice with roasted, broiled or fried meat, poultry or fish, fish cakes, or omelets.*
- *Press the rice into small ramekins, then turn out onto plates and garnish with fresh herbs.*
- *Serve as part of a meze meal (see page 42).*

Tomato Salad with Olives

Served with drinks, this salad makes a very good, light tapas dish and has all the flavors of the Mediterranean.

SERVES **2**

3 large tomatoes
½ medium red onion, sliced fine
A few black olives, pitted

VINAIGRETTE
8 Tbsp olive oil
3 Tbsp red wine vinegar
½ tsp garlic, chopped fine
½ Tbsp sugar
Salt and ground black pepper
Chives, chopped fine, to garnish

🍅 Slice the tomatoes in half horizontally. Arrange either in a large bowl with onion in between layers, or spread out on a large plate. Sprinkle with olives.

🍅 Combine the olive oil, red wine vinegar, garlic, and sugar in a bottle with a screw top. Shake hard until the dressing is emulsified. Season to taste, and shake again. Dredge the tomatoes with the dressing and serve garnished with chives.

🍅 If you wish to prepare the salad in advance, add the vinaigrette 20 minutes before required. The vinaigrette will keep in the refrigerator for up to two weeks.

Grilled Vegetables

These vegetables are great served on the side or as a meal in themselves with ciabatta or other breads to mop up the juices.

SERVES **4**

3 zucchini, cut into ¼-in slices
1 red bell pepper, cut into wide wedges or halves
1 yellow and 1 green bell pepper, cut into quarters
3 Tbsp extra virgin olive oil
5 garlic cloves, chopped
Juice of ½ lemon or 1 Tbsp balsamic or white
    wine vinegar

14 to 20 cherry tomatoes
Bamboo skewers, soaked in cold water for 30 minutes,
    or metal skewers
Salt and ground black pepper
2 to 3 Tbsp pesto or basil, chopped fine and puréed
    with a little garlic and olive oil

Combine the zucchini and peppers with the olive oil, garlic, and lemon or vinegar. Marinate for about 30 minutes if possible.

Meanwhile, thread the cherry tomatoes onto the skewers. Remove the zucchini and peppers from the marinade, saving the marinade to dress the vegetables afterward.

Grill the vegetables over a medium-high heat until lightly charred and brown in places and tender all the way through. Remove from the grill and return to the marinade. Let stand until the vegetables are cool enough to handle.

Meanwhile, grill the cherry tomatoes for about 5 minutes on each side or until slightly browned. Remove from the grill.

Dice the zucchini and peppers, and slice the tomatoes. Season, combine the juices with the pesto or basil, pour over the vegetables, and serve, dressed in a little olive oil if desired.

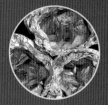

TO SAVOR

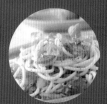

Tomato & Pepper Gazpacho

Served cold, this soup is a specialty of Andalusia and is traditionally made by pounding. In Spain, it is served as both an appetizer and as a tapas in tiny cups for sipping.

SERVES **4**

4 oz stale, country bread
¾ cup extra virgin olive oil
1½ cups ripe tomatoes, diced (see page 12)
1 green bell pepper, diced
4 garlic cloves, chopped fine
2 Tbsp sherry vinegar
Salt to taste

🍅 Cut or break the bread into bite-sized pieces, and place in the food processor or blender. Pour over enough cold water to cover it, leave for a moment or two, then drain.

🍅 Add the olive oil, tomatoes, bell pepper, garlic, sherry vinegar, and salt. Blend until a thick purée forms. Season to taste, and chill until ready to serve. Garnish as desired.

Garnishing Ideas

- *A crisp, crunchy garnish is a nice addition as this soup has a thick and creamy texture. Try diced, hard-cooked egg, crisp little croutons, and thin shreds of Spanish ham for a traditional gazpacho.*
- *Add shreds of fresh mint leaves and sweet cherry tomatoes, chopped fine.*

Tomato, Turkey, & Basil Lasagne

Use finely chopped turkey breast, or if preferred, chopped or ground chicken breast to make this tasty lasagne.

SERVES **4**

2 Tbsp olive oil

I large onion, peeled and finely chopped

2 to 3 garlic cloves, minced

12 oz ground turkey

Two 14-oz cans chopped tomatoes

Salt and ground black pepper

2 Tbsp chopped basil

6 to 8 fresh lasagne verdi sheets

2 cups zucchini, peeled, sliced lengthwise, and blanched

½ cup grated mozzarella cheese

Basil sprigs, to garnish

 Preheat the oven to 375°F, 10 minutes before baking the lasagne. Heat the oil in a large pan and sauté the onion and garlic for 5 minutes or until the onion is softened. Add the ground turkey and continue to sauté for a further 5 minutes or until sealed.

 Add the contents of the cans of tomatoes, bring to a boil, then reduce the heat and simmer for 10 minutes or until a thick consistency is formed. Season to taste and stir in the basil.

 Bring a large pan of water to a boil, add I tablespoon of salt, then drop in four lasagne sheets, one at a time. Cook for 2 to 3 minutes, ensuring that they do not stick together. Drain, lay them on clean dish towels, and pat dry. Repeat with the remaining lasagne sheets.

 Place about a third of the sauce in the base of an ovenproof dish and cover with a layer of blanched zucchini slices, then 3 to 4 lasagne sheets. Repeat the layering, finishing with a layer of sauce. Sprinkle with the grated cheese. Bake the lasagne in the oven for 20 to 25 minutes or until the cheese is golden. Serve garnished with basil sprigs.

Salmon & Tomato Packets

Wrap salmon fillets in foil and then cook them over a grill.
The aroma is wonderful.

SERVES **6**

Butter, for greasing
6 skinless salmon fillets, about 1½ in thick
6 fresh tomatoes
6 scallions, chopped
2 Tbsp olive oil
1 Tbsp lemon juice
1 tsp superfine sugar
Whole or chopped herbs, such as dill,
    cilantro, and parsley

Butter six large sheets of thick foil. Lay each salmon fillet on a sheet of foil. Cut each tomato into about 6 wedges and pile them on top of the salmon. Scatter the scallions over the tomatoes.

Whisk together the oil, lemon juice, and sugar. Drizzle it over the top of the salmon. Finally, add a few herb sprigs, or some chopped herbs, to each packet.

Close the packets, securing the seams well, then cook over medium-high heat for 8 to 10 minutes, turning the packets occasionally. Serve immediately.

Meatballs with Tomato & Eggplant Sauce

Simmer gently to prevent the meatballs from breaking up during cooking. Serve the meatballs with fresh vermicelli or tagliatelle and a selection of salad leaves.

SERVES **4**

MEATBALLS

1 lb ground lamb

6 scallions, chopped fine

1¼ cups fresh whole wheat bread crumbs

1 Tbsp tomato paste

½ tsp ground turmeric

Salt and ground black pepper

1 large egg, beaten

SAUCE

3 Tbsp olive oil

1 eggplant, cut into ½-in chunks

1 onion, diced fine

1 garlic clove, sliced fine

½ tsp ground turmeric

1 tsp ground cumin

4 cups canned chopped tomatoes

1 bay leaf

Salt and ground black pepper

8 to 10 basil leaves, torn

Parmesan (optional), to serve

 Mix all the ingredients for the meatballs together in a large bowl. Shape the mixture with wet hands into walnut-sized balls.

 To make the sauce, heat the oil in a large skillet, then add the eggplant and fry gently until lightly golden. Add the meatballs, together with the onion, garlic, turmeric, and cumin. Cook until the meatballs are browned all over. Add extra oil only if the meatballs are sticking.

 Add the tomatoes and bay leaf with the seasoning. Bring the mixture to a boil and let simmer gently for 20 minutes, then adjust the seasoning. Add the basil just before serving. Sprinkle the meatballs with Parmesan cheese, if desired.

Huevos Rancheros

Serve this egg, tomato, and pepper-based Mexican dish for brunch with pinto or black beans, rice, a little fresh salsa (see page 41), and a stack of warmed tortillas on the side.

SERVES **4**

1 onion, chopped

3 to 5 cloves garlic, chopped

3 to 4 Tbsp vegetable oil

1 to 2 green bell peppers, sliced thin

3 mild green chillies, roasted and sliced thin

1 to 2 green chillies, such as jalapeño, chopped (optional)

2 lb ripe tomatoes, diced (see page 12) or 14-oz can chopped tomatoes

Few oregano leaves, crushed

½ tsp cumin

Salt to taste

Pinch of sugar

½ tsp mild chili powder, or to taste

4 or 8 eggs (allow 1 or 2 per person)

4 or 8 tortillas (1 or 2 per person)

3 to 4 Tbsp chopped cilantro

🍅 Lightly sauté the onion and garlic in the oil until softened, then add the bell peppers, chillies, and tomatoes. Cook for a few minutes until the mixture forms a sauce.

🍅 Purée half the mixture with the oregano, cumin, salt, sugar, and chili powder, then return it to the pot with the reserved vegetables. Cook over medium heat until the sauce has reduced, stirring. Remove from the heat, season, and keep warm.

🍅 Meanwhile, poach or fry the eggs and warm the tortillas either in a microwave or on a lightly oiled heavy skillet. Place the eggs on top of the tortillas, with the warm sauce spooned over. Sprinkle with cilantro and serve immediately.

Picadillo

*Picadillo is a Latin American mixture of ground meat, browned
and simmered with spicy–sweet–savory ingredients. It is delicious rolled
into flour tortillas.*

SERVES **4**

1 onion, chopped

3 garlic cloves, chopped

2 Tbsp extra virgin olive oil

1 lb lean ground beef

¼ tsp cinnamon

¼ tsp cumin

¼ tsp cayenne pepper

Pinch of cloves

4 heaped Tbsp raisins

4 Tbsp toasted almonds or cashews

6 Tbsp sherry or dry, red wine

2 to 3 ripe tomatoes, diced (see page 12)

10 to 15 pimiento-stuffed green olives, sliced or halved

2 Tbsp tomato paste

1 to 2 Tbsp sugar, to taste

1 to 2 Tbsp red wine or sherry vinegar, to taste

2 Tbsp cilantro, chopped

Flour tortillas and cilantro sprigs, to serve

Sauté the onion and garlic in the olive oil until soft, then add the beef, and brown, sprinkling with the cinnamon, cumin, cayenne pepper, and cloves as it cooks.

Add the raisins, nuts, sherry or red wine, and bring to a boil. Cook until the sherry/wine has nearly evaporated, then add the tomatoes, olives, tomato paste, sugar, and vinegar, and cook together until the sauce is thick and flavorful.

Stir in the chopped cilantro, and serve in flour tortillas, garnished with cilantro sprigs.

Moroccan Chicken

The lemon used in this recipe permeates the chicken and olives add piquancy to the flavor. Try combinations of different olives for variety.

SERVES **4**

1 chicken, cut into serving pieces
1 Tbsp cumin
2 tsp paprika
½ tsp ginger
½ tsp turmeric
5 garlic cloves, chopped
Several handfuls of cilantro, chopped
Juice of 2 lemons

Ground black and cayenne pepper, to taste
3 to 5 Tbsp flour
4 tomatoes, chopped (either fresh or canned)
10 to 15 each (three types in total) of your
   chosen olives
1 lemon, cut into 6 wedges
¼ cup extra virgin olive oil
1 cup chicken broth
Extra lemon juice, to taste

Combine the chicken with cumin, paprika, ginger, turmeric, garlic, cilantro, lemon juice, and pepper. Place in a baking dish in a single layer. Leave to marinate for 30 minutes, then add the flour. Toss the ingredients together to coat well.

Heat the oven to 325°F. Add the tomatoes, olives, lemon wedges, olive oil, and broth to the dish. Bake uncovered for about an hour, or until the chicken is tender and a delicious sauce has formed. Add extra lemon juice, if desired.

Tip

- *There is little work in preparing this dish—it simmers away in the oven and is never less than delicious. However, the choice of ingredients is key. Spices are at the center of North African cuisine; it is therefore essential that the spices and herbs you use are absolutely fresh and of the highest quality.*

Pork Stifado in Foil

Based on a traditional Greek dish, the pork is cooked in foil on the grill instead of in a pot.

SERVES **4**

2 Tbsp olive oil, plus extra for brushing

1 medium onion, sliced thick

4 lean pork chops, each weighing about 8 oz

Salt and ground black pepper

2 plump garlic cloves, chopped fine

4 medium tomatoes, sliced

Ground allspice or cloves

4 sprigs of thyme

2 Tbsp red wine vinegar

🍅 Cut four large squares of thick foil, each large enough to make a loose packet around a pork chop. Brush each square lightly with olive oil.

🍅 Lay one quarter of the onion on each piece of foil and place a pork chop on top. Season, scatter the garlic on top, and add the tomato slices. Into each packet, sprinkle a pinch of allspice or cloves and add a sprig of thyme. Drizzle over the remaining 2 tablespoons oil and the vinegar. Fold the foil over and seal the packets well.

🍅 Cook over low-to-medium heat for about 30 to 40 minutes, turning occasionally, until the pork and onions are tender and golden brown.

NOODLE TIME

Tagliatelle with Vegetables in Fresh Tomato Sauce

The Mediterranean has an abundance of vegetables. Choose any combination you wish, but select compatible flavors and colors.

SERVES **4**

1 red and 1 yellow bell pepper, seeded

¼ stick butter

1 large onion, peeled and cut into thin wedges

2 to 3 garlic cloves, peeled and crushed

1½ cups zucchini, diced

8 Tbsp dry white wine

1 lb plum tomatoes, peeled, seeded, and chopped (see page 12)

2 Tbsp tomato paste

2 Tbsp chopped basil

Salt and ground black pepper

1 lb fresh tagliatelle and freshly shaved Parmesan cheese, to serve

🍅 Preheat the broiler to high and broil the peppers for 10 minutes. Remove from the broiler and place in a plastic bag. Leave for 10 minutes, then peel and cut into strips.

🍅 Melt the butter in a large heavy saucepan and sauté the onion and garlic for 5 minutes. Add the zucchini and sauté for 2 minutes. Stir in the wine, chopped tomatoes, and tomato paste. Bring the sauce to a boil, reduce the heat, and cook for 5 to 8 minutes. Stir in the sliced peppers and basil, and season to taste. Continue to simmer gently while cooking the pasta.

🍅 Cook the tagliatelle in plenty of salted boiling water for 1 to 2 minutes or until *al dente*. Drain and add the pasta to the sauce, toss lightly, and serve with Parmesan cheese.

Pasta with Raw Tomato Sauce, Basil, & Goat Cheese

This recipe is the classic combination of hot pasta with raw tomatoes, rich with olive oil, basil, garlic, and a crumbling of goat cheese for fresh piquancy.

SERVES **4**

10 very ripe, juicy tomatoes, diced
  (see page 12)
Salt, to taste
Few drops of balsamic vinegar
3 garlic cloves, chopped
4 to 6 Tbsp extra virgin olive oil
Several handfuls of basil, coarsely torn
Few pinches of chili flakes (optional)
12 oz pasta of choice
1 cup goat cheese, crumbled

 Combine the tomatoes with several pinches of salt, balsamic vinegar, garlic, most of the olive oil (reserve 1 tablespoon), and basil (plus the chili flakes, if using). Let sit for at least 30 minutes, or preferably chill in the refrigerator for several hours.

 When ready to serve, cook the pasta for 1 to 2 minutes until *al dente*, then drain and toss with the goat cheese and remaining olive oil. Add to the sauce and serve immediately.

Pasta with Fresh Tomatoes

Make this recipe when ripe plum tomatoes are available. Serve with crusty Italian bread.

SERVES **4**

2 Tbsp olive oil

½ stick butter

I small onion, chopped fine

I garlic clove, crushed

I ½ lb plum tomatoes, peeled, seeded, and cut
  into chunks (see page 12)

I tsp superfine sugar

Salt and ground black pepper

4 Tbsp chopped parsley

2 Tbsp chopped tarragon or
  I Tbsp chopped thyme

Freshly cooked pasta and torn basil,
  to serve

Heat the olive oil and butter together in a heavy saucepan. Add the onion and garlic. Cook, stirring, for 15 minutes, or until the onion has softened. Stir in the tomatoes, sugar, and seasoning to taste. Cook, stirring, until the tomatoes are hot. Stir in the parsley and tarragon or thyme. Toss the mixture with freshly cooked pasta, then gently toss in the basil.

Serving Idea

- *This pasta sauce can be served with any variety of pasta—long thin pasta such as spaghetti, or small shapes—orecchiette for example.*

Spaghetti with Tomato & Clams

Tiny clams tossed on a sea of tomato-based spaghetti sauce is a Neapolitan favorite. Mussels can be substituted in place of clams.

SERVES **4**

2¼ lb fresh clams in their shells, or mussels
    (removed from shells)
8 garlic cloves, chopped
½ cup extra virgin olive oil
Several pinches of hot, red-pepper flakes
½ cup dry white wine
1 cup puréed tomatoes
1 Tbsp tomato paste
Sea salt to taste
Pinch sugar
Several large pinches of dried oregano, crumbled
1 lb fresh spaghetti
2 to 3 Tbsp chopped parsley

Discard any clams or mussels that are open. Cover the clams or mussels with cold, salted water and leave for 30 to 60 minutes to clean. Remove and drain.

Sauté the seafood with half the garlic in olive oil for about 5 minutes, then add the hot red-pepper flakes and wine. Cook over high heat to evaporate. Add the tomatoes, tomato paste, remaining garlic, salt, sugar, and oregano. Cover and cook over medium heat until the seafood shells open, about 10 minutes. Discard any shells that have remained closed.

Cook the spaghetti in boiling salted water for 1 to 2 minutes until *al dente*, then drain and toss with a few tablespoons of the sauce. Pour the pasta into bowls and top with the remaining sauce and seafood. Sprinkle with parsley and serve immediately.

Pasta with Tomato & Tuna

Tuna is a classic ingredient in Italy. In this recipe canned tuna is actually more authentic than fresh.

SERVES **4** TO **6**

1 onion, chopped

5 garlic cloves, chopped

6 Tbsp extra virgin olive oil

2½ lb diced tomatoes (see page 12)

2 Tbsp tomato paste (optional)

Salt, ground black pepper, and a pinch of sugar

Pinch of oregano and/or marjoram

6½-oz can tuna, drained

1 lb fresh spaghetti

3 Tbsp capers, salted

10 to 15 black olives

3 Tbsp parsley, chopped

Few Tbsp of toasted bread crumbs (optional)

Lightly sauté the onion and half the garlic in the olive oil until softened, then add the tomatoes and cook over medium heat until the tomatoes are juicy. Add the tomato paste, if needed, for extra flavor. Season with salt, pepper, and sugar and add a pinch of herbs to taste. Add the tuna to the sauce, and heat through.

Meanwhile, cook the pasta in rapidly boiling, salted water for 1 to 2 minutes until *al dente*, then drain. Pour half the sauce into the pasta, and toss together with the capers and olives, then toss with the rest of the sauce. Sprinkle with parsley and toasted bread crumbs (if using), and serve.

Quick Tomato Sauce

This sauce is ideal when time is critical and you are relying on ingredients you have on hand. It is an excellent sauce to use with filled pasta as well as layered dishes.

MAKES 1 CUP

2 Tbsp olive oil

1 large onion, peeled and grated

14-oz can chopped tomatoes

Salt and ground black pepper

Few dashes of Tabasco sauce

1 lb fresh pasta and freshly shaved Parmesan cheese, to serve

Heat the oil in a large heavy saucepan and sauté the onion for 5 minutes. Add the canned tomatoes and sauté gently for 10 minutes. Season and add Tabasco sauce to taste, cover with a lid, and remove from the heat.

Meanwhile, cook the pasta in plenty of boiling, salted water for 1 to 2 minutes until *al dente*. Drain, then return to the pan. Add the sauce to the cooked pasta. Heat through for 2 minutes, tossing lightly. Serve immediately, sprinkled with fresh shavings of Parmesan cheese.

Serving Ideas

- *Instead of smothering stuffed pasta shapes with the sauce, ladle the sauce on to a plate, then arrange the pasta on top. This is ideal for strong-colored sauces, such as tomato. Add a herb garnish to the pasta.*
- *An alternative method of serving pasta and sauce is to put half the pasta in a warmed dish, top with the sauce then add the remaining pasta. Add a garnish of herbs or other suitable ingredients (shaved cheese, olives, pepper slices, and so on), then take the dish to the table. This works well with attractive pasta shapes.*

Butter & Tomato Sauce

Beefsteak tomatoes are extremely tasty. Choose fresh, ripe tomatoes for this simple, but delicious, sauce.

MAKES **2** CUPS

1½ lb ripe beefsteak tomatoes, peeled (see page 12)
¾ stick unsalted butter
6 shallots, peeled and chopped fine
3 Tbsp basil leaves
Salt and ground black pepper
1 lb fresh pasta, basil leaves, and freshly grated
  Parmesan cheese, to serve

Seed and dice the tomatoes (see page 12). Melt 4 tablespoons of butter in a large heavy saucepan and gently sauté the shallots for 5 minutes or until softened. Add the remaining butter and the tomatoes and continue to sauté gently for 5 to 8 minutes or until the tomatoes begin to break down. Stir in the basil leaves with seasoning to taste. Cover and remove from the heat.

Meanwhile, cook the pasta in plenty of salted, boiling water for 1 to 2 minutes until *al dente*. Drain and add to the tomato sauce. Toss lightly and serve immediately, garnished with extra basil leaves. Serve with freshly grated Parmesan cheese.

Sun-dried Tomato with Black Olive Sauce

This is a robust sauce that is ideally suited to the thicker ribbons of pasta, such as tagliatelle, or shapes such as penne or garganelli.

MAKES 1 CUP

2 Tbsp olive oil

1 Tbsp sun-dried tomato oil

1 medium onion, peeled and chopped fine

8 sun-dried tomatoes in oil, chopped fine

2 garlic cloves, peeled and crushed

2 celery stems, trimmed and chopped fine

2 oz pancetta, chopped

½ cup black olives, pitted and chopped

1 Tbsp tomato paste

1¼ cups vegetable broth

Few sprigs of marjoram

Salt and ground black pepper

1 lb fresh pasta, extra sprigs of marjoram,
    and freshly grated Parmesan cheese, to serve

🍅 Heat the olive oil and sun-dried tomato oil in a heavy saucepan and sauté the onion, sun-dried tomatoes, garlic, celery, and pancetta for 5 minutes. Stir in half the olives.

🍅 Blend the tomato paste with a little of the broth, then stir into the pan with the remaining broth and the marjoram. Bring to a boil and let simmer for 10 minutes. Cool, then pass through a food processor and return to the pan. Season to taste and add the remaining olives. Cover with a lid and remove from the heat.

🍅 Meanwhile, cook the pasta in plenty of salted boiling water for 1 to 2 minutes or until *al dente*. Drain well, then add the tomato sauce; toss lightly. Serve immediately, scattered with torn marjoram sprigs and Parmesan cheese.

IN THE MIX

Lebanese Salad

This salad of stale bread and vegetables originates from Lebanon. It is characteristically dressed with lots of olive oil and lemon, and is very refreshing.

SERVES **4**

1 large or 2 small cucumbers, diced

3 ripe tomatoes, diced (see page 12)

1 green bell pepper, diced

About 8 Tbsp each: chopped mint, cilantro,
   and parsley

3 scallions, sliced thin

1 tsp salt

3 garlic cloves, chopped

6 Tbsp extra virgin olive oil

Juice of 3 lemons

1 tsp sumac (if available)

3 to 4 pita breads, stale and lightly toasted,
   then broken into pieces

Combine the cucumbers, tomatoes, bell pepper, herbs, scallions, salt, garlic, olive oil, lemon juice, and sumac in a bowl. Chill for at least one hour. Just before serving, toss with the broken pita breads.

Mixed Bean Chili

Chili con carne has always been a warming favorite and this recipe is the vegetarian version. It is a healthful and satisfying meal.

SERVES **4**

16-oz can borlotti, kidney, black-eyed,
   or pinto beans, drained
14-oz can chopped tomatoes
1 Tbsp tomato paste
1 onion, halved and sliced
⅔ cup potatoes, cubed
1 green bell pepper, seeded and chopped
¾ cup baby corn, halved
2 green chillies, seeded and chopped
1 tsp chili powder
2 garlic cloves, crushed
⅔ cup vegetable broth
Chopped parsley, to garnish
Brown rice or baked potatoes, to serve

Place all the ingredients except the garnish in a large heavy saucepan and bring to a boil. Reduce the heat, cover the pan, and let simmer for 45 minutes or until all of the vegetables are cooked and the juices have thickened slightly. Stir the chili occasionally while cooking.

Garnish with parsley and serve with brown rice or baked potatoes.

Mixed Bean Chili

Rock 'n' Roll Bagel

A rich combination of leeks, tomatoes, and mushrooms with Roquefort cheese.

SERVES **2**

2 Tbsp olive oil
1 clove of garlic, crushed
1 Tbsp chopped rosemary
½ leek, thinly sliced
2 oz mushrooms, quartered
2 oz cherry tomatoes, quartered
2 oz Roquefort cheese, crumbled
2 bagels
Butter or margarine, for spreading
Rosemary sprigs, to garnish

Heat the oil in a frying pan and add the garlic and chopped rosemary. Cook for about 1 minute.

Add the leek and mushrooms and continue to cook for about 5 minutes, or until the vegetables are lightly browned. Add the cherry tomatoes and Roquefort cheese and cook for a further minute.

Meanwhile, cut the bagels in half horizontally and toast. Butter the cut surfaces. Serve on individual plates with the Roquefort filling. Garnish with sprigs of rosemary.

Pasta & Ratatouille

Canned tomatoes are used in this recipe but if you prefer you can substitute 1½ pounds fresh peeled tomatoes and an extra tablespoon of tomato paste.

SERVES **4**

1 medium eggplant, trimmed and sliced

Salt

4 Tbsp olive oil

1 large onion, peeled and sliced thin

2 to 4 garlic cloves, peeled and chopped

1½ cups sliced zucchini

Two 14-oz cans chopped tomatoes

1 Tbsp tomato paste

6 Tbsp red wine

Ground black pepper

1 Tbsp chopped oregano

1 Tbsp chopped flat-leaf parsley

¾ cup button mushrooms, wiped and halved

10 oz fresh orecchiette and ¾ cup sliced
    mozzarella cheese, to serve

Layer the eggplant in a colander, sprinkling between each layer with salt. Leave for 30 minutes. Drain, rinse well in cold water, and pat dry. Heat the oil in a large heavy saucepan and sauté the eggplant, onion, garlic, and zucchini for 5 to 8 minutes or until softened. Add extra oil, if necessary, as the eggplant will tend to soak it up.

Add the tomatoes. Blend the tomato paste with the wine. Stir it into the pan with the black pepper, oregano, parsley, and mushrooms. Bring to a boil, reduce the heat, cover, and let simmer for 15 minutes.

Meanwhile, cook the pasta in plenty of boiling salted water for 1 to 2 minutes or until *al dente*. Drain and place in the base of an ovenproof gratin dish. Pour over the sauce and top with the cheese. Place under a medium-hot broiler and cook for 5 to 8 minutes or until the cheese has melted and is golden.

Maltagliati with Lamb & Chives

Any ribbon-like pasta works well in this recipe as it coats easily with the sauce. Serve sprinkled with Parmesan cheese and chives.

SERVES **4**

3 Tbsp olive oil

2 garlic cloves, peeled and chopped fine

I large onion, peeled and chopped

10 oz lean lamb, trimmed and chopped fine

14-oz can chopped tomatoes

I Tbsp tomato paste

4 Tbsp red wine

I Tbsp snipped chives

Salt and ground black pepper

I lb fresh maltagliati, 2 to 3 Tbsp freshly grated
   Parmesan cheese and extra snipped chives, to serve

Heat the oil in a heavy saucepan and sauté the garlic and onion for 5 minutes or until softened. Add the lamb and continue to sauté for 5 minutes, stirring frequently, until browned.

Add the tomatoes, tomato paste blended with 2 tablespoons water, and the wine. Bring to a boil, reduce the heat, cover with a lid, and let simmer for 40 minutes or until a thick sauce is formed. Add the chives and season to taste. Continue to simmer for 5 minutes while cooking the pasta.

Cook the pasta in plenty of salted boiling water for I to 2 minutes or until *al dente*. Drain and return to the pan. Add the sauce, toss lightly, and serve.

Mediterranean Salad

This colorful salad is a great dish to serve as an appetizer.

SERVES **4**

1¼ cups vegetable broth

1 onion, chopped fine

1 garlic clove, crushed

¼ cup dry white wine

4 tomatoes, peeled and chopped
   (see page 12)

Juice of 1 lime

1 Tbsp cider vinegar

2 tsp tomato paste

1 tsp fennel seeds

1 tsp mustard seeds

1 cup button mushrooms, quartered

2 oz French beans, trimmed

1 zucchini, sliced

Ground black pepper

Basil sprig, to garnish

Heat the broth in a large heavy saucepan and cook the onion and garlic for 3 to 4 minutes. Add the wine, tomatoes, lime juice, vinegar, tomato paste, fennel, and mustard seeds and the vegetables. Bring the mixture to a boil, reduce the heat and let simmer for 20 minutes or until the vegetables are just cooked. Season with black pepper to taste.

Transfer the mixture to a serving dish. Cover and chill for at least 1 hour. Garnish with basil, then serve.

Tip

• *Any combination of vegetables would be delicious steeped in this tomato and garlic sauce. You could use eggplant, roasted bell peppers, leeks, scallions, or artichokes.*

Mediterranean Vegetable Risotto

This risotto makes a stunning main course. Serve simply with herb or cheese bread.

SERVES **4**

1 medium eggplant
2 medium zucchini
1 red bell pepper
2 medium tomatoes
1 red onion
2 garlic cloves
6 Tbsp olive oil

2 Tbsp chopped fresh rosemary or 2 tsp dried
5 cups vegetable broth
1 medium onion, finely chopped
2 cups arborio rice
⅔ cup dry white wine
Salt and ground black pepper
⅓ cup diced halloumi or feta cheese
Rosemary, to garnish

First prepare the vegetables. Trim and dice the eggplant into 1-inch pieces. Trim and slice the zucchini. Seed and dice the pepper into 1-inch cubes. Quarter the tomatoes. Peel and cut the red onion into eight wedges. Peel and thinly slice the garlic.

Place all the vegetables in a bowl and gently stir in 5 tablespoons of olive oil and the rosemary until well mixed. Preheat the broiler to a hot setting. Pile the vegetables into the broiler pan and cook the vegetables for 8 to 10 minutes, turning frequently, until lightly charred and tender. Set aside.

Pour the broth into a saucepan and bring to a boil. Reduce the heat to a gentle simmer.

Meanwhile, heat the remaining oil in a large saucepan and gently fry the onion for 2 to 3 minutes until softened. Add the rice and cook, stirring, for 2 minutes until well coated in the onion mixture.

Add the wine and cook gently, stirring, until absorbed. Ladle in the broth gradually, until all the liquid is absorbed and the rice is thick, creamy, and tender. Keep the heat moderate. This will take about 25 minutes. Season well.

Gently mix in the prepared vegetables and heat through for 2 to 3 minutes until hot. Serve sprinkled with the cheese and garnish with rosemary.

Garlic Cheese with Sun-dried Tomatoes

Any firm, moist garlic cheese will work well in this recipe. Try Teifi, Gapron or Gaperon—the strong, French, dome-shaped, peppered cheese.

SERVES **4**

8 sun-dried tomatoes

¾ cup full-bodied red wine

1 small onion, chopped fine

2 Tbsp chopped oregano

2 bay leaves

Salt and ground black pepper

4 Tbsp olive oil

2 cups garlic-flavored cheese, cut into cubes

2 pickled walnuts, chopped

Fresh pasta and 4 Tbsp chopped parsley, to serve

🍅 Snip the sun-dried tomatoes into small pieces with kitchen scissors. Place them in a small heavy saucepan with the wine, onion, oregano, and bay leaves. Season to taste. Heat gently until simmering. Cover the pan and cook for 5 minutes. Remove from the heat and let stand for 2 hours.

🍅 Add the olive oil, cheese, and walnuts to the tomato mixture. Stir well and leave to marinate overnight. To serve, strain the liquid from the cheese mixture into a large saucepan. Bring to a boil and boil hard for 3 minutes, whisking occasionally. Pour the hot dressing over freshly cooked pasta. Add the strained cheese and tomato mixture, and the parsley. Toss well and serve immediately.

Index